642

THINGS TO DRAW

YOUNG ARTIST'S EDITION

BY 826 VALENCIA

chronicle books · san francisco

ISBN 978-1-4521-5066-6

Manufactured in China.

FSC
www.fsc.org
MIX
Paper from
responsible sources
FSC™ C104723

Design by Eloise Leigh.
Typesetting by Kris Branco.

10 9 8 7 6 5 4 3 2

Chronicle Books LLC
680 Second Street
San Francisco, California 94107

Chronicle Books—we see things differently.
Become part of our community at www.chroniclekids.com.

Chronicle books and gifts are available at special quantity discounts to corporations, professional
associations, literacy programs, and other organizations. For details and discount information,
please contact our premiums department at corporatesales@chroniclebooks.com or at
1-800-759-0190.

AT 826 VALENCIA, creativity is of utmost importance. It is a well-known fact that our cranky editors, Mr. and Mrs. Blue, will not approve stories that they have heard before. You will not find Cinderellas or Spider-Mans or Harry Potters at 826. When elementary school students visit our writing center in San Francisco, they write stories and publish books in just two hours. We ask middle school students to give us their unique take on current events when writing our in-house newspaper, which means researching hoverboards and raccoon populations. And we encourage our high school students to share their memories and stories with us, which we then publish in beautiful books and magazines. We do all of this because we believe that young people—like you!—have important and brilliant stories to share.

From porcupines with blue Mohawks to tiptoeing lies, our students' stories are uniquely theirs. Everything you find in this book came from an 826 Valencia student. You might find some of these things funny, ridiculous, or whimsical, but they are—without a doubt—creative. Where else will you find a frozen dog with a mustache? We insist on creativity when telling stories, because we know that our students can be artists. We know that all kids can be artists.

This book is full of ideas to spark your imagination and encourage self-expression, just as we do every day at 826 Valencia. You can start this book at the beginning and work through it one page at a time, or you can start at the back and work backward, or you can open it up at random and start there. You can draw with pencils or pens. You can draw in color or in black and white. You can fill every last space with drawings or you can leave some space blank. It is your choice, but please think about it and choose carefully. Make every choice a creative one. After all, it's your vision.

As you blanket these pages with art, you might find that one particular image won't leave your mind—one that demands to come off the page. Don't let your creativity be limited to this book; let these pages serve as the inspiration for your creativity. Maybe you'll be inspired to write a novel or paint a mural or make a film that turns into the next summer blockbuster hit!

To create these drawing prompts, we looked at all the stories that have ever been written at 826 Valencia. These stories were written by students in schools, workshops, after-school programs, field trips, and all of our other free programs, which couldn't have happened without the support of our volunteers and community. If you are interested in getting involved or supporting our organization, please visit 826valencia.org.

Now start drawing!

EMMA PEOPLES
826 Valencia Programs Assistant

CONTRIBUTORS FROM THE FOLLOWING SCHOOLS

Second graders at Alamo Elementary School
Second graders at Cleveland Elementary School
Second graders at Jose Ortega Elementary School
Second graders at Junipero Serra Elementary School
Second graders at Cesar Chavez Elementary School
Third graders at Buena Vista Horace Mann School
Third graders at Cesar Chavez Elementary School
Third graders at Dr. Charles R. Drew Alternative Elementary School
Third graders at Colonial Acres Elementary
Third graders at Leonard R. Flynn Elementary School
Fourth graders at Buena Vista Horace Mann School
Fourth graders at Charles Armstrong School
Fourth graders at Glen Park School
Fourth graders at Harvey Milk Civil Rights Academy
Fourth graders at Paul Revere Elementary
Fourth graders at Sanchez Elementary School
Fourth graders at Visitacion Valley
Fourth/Fifth graders at San Francisco Community School
Fifth graders at Buena Vista Horace Mann School
Fifth graders at Hillcrest Elementary School

KIDS WHO DRAW FOR THE PIRATE STORE

Abigail Giron Jimenez
Adela Kelemen
Ajay Balaoro
Alan Arreola
Alena Byer
Alex Gomez
Alex Lim
Alexander Castellanos
Alexis Aleman
Alexis Gamez
Alicia Morales
Allison Lee
Alvin Yu
Amberley Laverick
Amiel Franz del Campo
Ana Da Cruz
Anahi Zarate
Andrea Alcantara
Angel Rodriguez
Angelina Armond
Angelo Gonzales
Antonio Curtis
Antony Antunez
Ardelia Martinez
Ariana Gomez
Arwelie Caballero
Ashante Williams
Ashely Asberry
Ashly Nava
Asta Dreir
Austin Lewis
Avi Saha
Axel Bonilla
Aziza Hayes
Azriel Becerra
Bianca Vasquez
Bichang Cui
Brandon Ly
Brandon Ramos
Brandon Yañez
 Rodriguez
Brenda Hernandez
Brendan Sasso
Brian Moore
Brisa Tortolero
Calvin Tan
Cameron Samayoa
Camila Mora
Carlos Flores
Carlos Rivera
Carmen Demartis
Cassandra Beautler
Celine Beltran
Cesar Martinez
Chase Louie
Chesdon Lee
Chloe Villegas
Chloe White
Christian Zuleta Madrid
Cindy Antunez
Cindy Saavedra

Claire Williams
Clayton Anderson
Crisyeyda Altamirano
Daisy Guzman
Daniel Aguilar
Daniel Delgado
Daphne Gonzalez
David Campos
David Melone
David Pimentel
Delilah Kaden
Desiree Martinez
Destiny Venegas
Devon Kearney
Diana Chicas
Diego Avila
Diego Cristerna
Diego Gambala
Diego Solano
Diego Talbot
Dominic Valle
Eda Kaban
Eliette Chanezon
Elijah Romero-
 Antoniades
Emcy Angel Canlas
Emily Cruz
Emily Sobelman
Emma Hyndman
Emma Mayer
Emma Sherwood-Forbes
Eric Argueta
Eric Ng
Erica Kunisaki
Erick Meza-Castro
Esteban Sanchez
Estefany Villanueva
Esther Vargas
Eva Melin-Gompper
Evelyn Flores
Evelyn Michaus
Fatima Santos
Felix Keeler
Fernanda Mercado
Franchesca Lopez
Francisco "Panchito"
 Perez
Freily Agreda
Gabriel Peña Sanchez
Gage Cross
Genesis Laguna
George Mejia-Cuellar
Gigi Henriquez
Gina Cardenas
Giovani
Giselle Maldonado
Giuseppe Pacheco
Gonzalo Duque Leiva
Grace Bayne
Guadalupe Campos
Gustavo Torres

Han Luu
Hector Ramos Diaz
Henry Rodriguez
Ibraheem Muhammad
Isabell Rusitzky
Isabella Lavine
Isaiah Ruiz
Jackson Rose
Jacobi Napili
Jacqueline Gutierrez
Jaden Lüschen
Jalin Washington
Janine Lacap
Jasmin Gonzalez
Jasmine Hernandez
Jason Cazarez
Jason Tan
Jasper M. Bettag
Jay-Ling Lira
Jayden Foston
Jaye Evans
Jennifer Herrera Silva
Jessica Berrios
Jessica Lo
Jessica Ngai
Jesús Islas
Jhonna Herrera Mendez
Joanna Hernandez
Jocelyn C. Almendares
Jon Dowell
Jonathan Cruz-Umanzor
Jonathan Marquez
Jonathan Ramirez
Jorge Avalos
Jose Perez
Jose Poot Vera
Josep Mungia
Joseph Broussard
Josue Ramirez
Joyce Perez
Juan Ramirez
Judy Wu
Julian Merino
Julian Trujillo
Julieta Roll
Julisa Vargas
June Imler
Justin Sione
Kai-Fan Tsang
Kalena So
Kamiyah Colbert
Karla Hernandez
Katherine Gomez Son
Keanu Urrutia
Kehau Lyons
Keily Ponce
Ken Xu
Kevin Cruz-Umanzor
Kimberly Suazo
Kimberly T. Laud
Kimi Flores

Kina Paul
Laura Pogio
Layla Durrani
Leonel Campos
Leslie Franco
Leslie Marinez
Lilian Delcid
Lizbeth Lopez
Lluvia Quintero
Lorraine Piercy
Lucia Mena
Lucie Pereira
Lucio Alfaro
Makayla Ferrell
Maria Solares Horsfield
Maria Torres
Maria Verduzco
Mariah Evans Zink
Marjorie Hernandez
Marlon Hernandez
Marvin Guerra
Matthew de Andrade
Matthew Dunn
Maurice Jones
Maya Chatterjee
Meethana Singh
Melina Chamorro
Meyonna Payne
Michael Bura
Michael Chung
Michael Manalo
Michelle Garcia
Michelle Santos
Miguel Nava
Miguel Nunez
Miguel Sandoval Segura
Molly Ugarte
Monica Chan
Mons Skoglund
Morgan Berg
Myckel Martinez
Nakai Cristerna
Natalia Gonzalez
Niamey Harris
Nick Dias
Nicole Navarro
Noe Campos
Nolan Pita
Odalis Alvarez
Oliver Hernandez
Oliver Paddock
Omar Herrera
Pablo Barrera
Paola Flores
Paolo Yumol
Patrick Zhang
Radford Leung
Ramiro Hurtado
Reilly Pehling
Richard Brown
Rita Tapia

Robert Garcia
Robert Sotelo
Roberto Delgado
Robinson Martinez
Roisin McLaughlin
Romero Perez
Ronald Sullivan
Roz LaBean
Ruby Penn
Sabine Dahi
Sachiel Fregric Nunaz
 Michael Rosen
Sahid Rizo Castillo
Sally Mao
Sam Gallerani
Sami Bryon-Duskis
Samson Gong
Saul Martinez
Savonne Thompson
Sebastiaan Leddy
Selena Hernandez
 Chase
Sergio Magana
Sharina Gutierrez
 Cauich
Shengyi Wen
Shuzhen Zhang
Siri Young
Stella Chin
Stephany Pescador
Syeda Mohsin
Tamicka Price-Baker
Tasha Angstadt
Tenisha Chapman
Teodoro Kimbal-Directo
Thomson Corvin
Tien Ortman
Tiffany Lee
Tiuli Kulishi
Trevor Britton
Tyiera Marshall
Uriel Delgado
Vanessa Perez
Victoria Chen
Warren Reed
Wayman Ng
Wing Yiu
Yaseen Elhamaki
Yayi Ruan
Yesenia Cruz
Yingyi Mo
Yuridiana Cleofas
Yutong Chen
Yuyan Yu
Yvonne Chung
Zenay Clemmons
Zi Ye
Zoe Morgan-Weinman
Zola Rosenfeld
Zora Rosenberg

a magical golden bag

---

baking Olympics

the kraken

a wolf and vampire couple

purple lightning

bean and cheese pupusas

puppy pajamas

a hamster in a catapult wearing a helmet

a big pink photobooth

a porcupine with a blue Mohawk

a pasture of lilies and carrots

a friendly one-eyed alien with six arms

a clown with rainbow-colored hair

spider socks

a monster mask

a skeleton army

Twizzler cupcakes

a diamond boat

magical hats

a robot superhero

laser eyes

a dance battle

Lollipop Kingdom

a chocolate forest

one hundred handfuls of sugar

a scarlet macaw

---

a coconut slingshot

a pet polar bear

a laser cannon

---

living cookie birds

---

a park in Peru

you, as a traveling balloon

a train with wings

a cheetah, trained as a soldier

a misunderstood, adolescent orca

a ten-minute slide ride

a robot with two fighting heads

a dog and pizza hamburger with wings

draggony (part dragon, part bunny)

a vampire-robot-tiger

a lion angel

an alien pony

pizza police

a fire-shooting flamenco dancer

mutant butterflies

Santa's super-unicorn hero

a zombie unicorn

kitdragig (part kitty, part dragon, part pig)

a cowboy dancing with an elephant

---

the hot sauce planet

a tiger woman

---

running through plants

---

a crocodile selling blue glitter to color the sky

a unicorn rainbow explosion cake with rainbow sprinkles

Chompy, the dinosaur college student

a happy tiger in a city

dollar bills crashing to the ground

walking candy

garbage flowers

dofi (part dog, part fish)

the planet Guaka Guaka

---

a cupcake chainsaw

Ice Cream Land

Unicornlandia

---

zombies in the town of Lollipop

a boy made of cookies

Cloudland

dancing light

---

a reflection in the mirror

---

a lot of balloons

cereal in the mornings

a curly-feathered crow

a sunken treasure chest

invisible cities

life at its fullest

Zeus's master bolt

sitting on the floor

mist rivulets gathered on cars

the bottom of the ocean

smelly creatures

raccoon problems

furry animals that look like bandits

a chilling Arctic freeze

dancing dogs

a BLT that fell apart

an electric blue rosebush that towers over you

strands of frozen metal hair

a crazy jungle full of giant animals and tiny animals

an elephant and a monkey

a monster in your house

tippy-toeing down the stairs

---

playing hide-and-seek

confused people | a soft patch of grass

dancing to the music of your past

two monsters eating salad

an oddball selection of musicians

a house that is surprised

trapped in a storm

a crowd gathered in amazement

a blueberry sky

a nightmare

spilled coffee

jumping in the street

a faraway castle

clouds raining down magic crystals

a real gold robot suit

---

dogs that can fly

wizards that have big elephant ears

hair like icicles

a Froot Loop among Cheerios

a famous koala

splattered Oreos

a mind sharp as razors

---

an avocado wearing a coat

---

the feathered serpent that poses in the moonlight at Chichén Itzá

plantains, a slice of cheese, tomatoes, cabbage, onion, and lime

a Pokemon battle

stolen grapes

a colossal line at airport security

a wild uncle

four square on a playground

a Catholic school

show-offs and cool guys

a nail polish party

Spanish class

recess

butterflies flying around my stomach

a wedding at city hall

a short basketball coach with a buzz cut and a star shaved on the side of his head barbecuing a pig in the backyard

a place full of strollers and children

Crunchy, the fairly burnt toast monster

a puppy's head sticking out of a backpack

---

a day at Six Flags

a praying turtle

a wooden hut in the forest

a zebra named Larry

a hippo eating a sandwich

a princess with long curly hair like Rapunzel

a curious baby panda

a little kid on a pirate ship

elves baking cookies

---

an eel's castle

an ugly, green wizard

---

a rainforest cake

a potion that makes you invisible

a fire-red race car

marshmallows on the moon

a walking cookie named Bites

a super cobra

a squirrel in a shopping mall

a great-grandmother gardening

a pizza that has been in the oven for too long

time going as fast as a rocket ship

cows and pigs on a ranch

getting grounded

a mall security guard

frozen crabs

dancing taste buds

seeing a ghost

riding a bike indoors

angels' wings

a great red ocean

old bones

B.N.F.: Best Neighbors Forever

a messy cafeteria

a hot day in Africa

big bugs and rats

dodging fireballs

---

a better world

fighting an anaconda   corn in a cornfield eggs sunny–side up

a monkey chasing a turtle

a best friend handshake

---

a car on the top of a mountain overlooking a city

a window into the soul

---

an embarrassed face

---

a sneaky chameleon

a light green T. rex with yellow spots

the crown of knowledge

a cupcake field

a panda on a dusty, gigantic mountain

golden leaves falling off a tree

shadows racing up the walls of a house

a field of grain turning dark yellow

people singing after sunset

firecrackers going off

a smelly, sweaty bus

a thin curtain of fog that covers the sky

a puzzle with missing pieces

little birds singing

---

sellers shouting in a crowded marketplace

waking up as a zombie

your random junk drawer

a yellow and black cheetah running

a newborn ladybug

a bear getting ready for bed

a Jell-O maker | crumbs on the floor

a bearded lumberjack | a light pink baby

pictures covered in spiderwebs

a flowing dress made out of fluffy, humongous clouds

a pizza jail

cakes baking in the kitchen

lava, rocks, and glass

---

a star excreting candy

---

an elephantine cow

five chocolates with whipped cream and strawberries and sweet honey on top of a pancake

---

a crazy apple tree

smelly cheese inside a gym sock

a tomato splattered against a freshly painted white wall

a ball bouncing

two sweet watermelons

a troll gulping down yummy villagers

you, in space

a tap dancer in a history class

the top of a mountain at dusk

a sleeping koala

a dad going grocery shopping

a little minion happy to do work

a diving penguin

a rabbit with a jacket

a hologram

shoelaces on brand-new sneakers

---

the familiar smell of salami from yesterday's sandwich

a chocolate party

a weird-looking mustache

a swarm of bees

bullets of electricity

dirty hand stains

a red bird that looks like a strawberry

---

a cell phone dreaming when it's turned off

a kid alone in a redwood forest

a family of wolves

a German shepherd police dog

drawings carved into a desk

a black hole pulling you in

an angry tiger

---

a vanilla ice-cream scoop lying on the sidewalk

confetti falling from the sky

a beautiful lily

two wiener dogs

---

a house carved into the side of a mountain

a car that drives on water

a ball of fire

Cleopatra

an endless mountain

a crazy cat that hasn't been fed

a sleepy dog

the oldest turtle in the world

a person running on the moon

a basketball player dunking the ball in the hoop | a grove of tall pine trees

a shy moon

---

waves crashing

a jungle of brightly colored houses

a fragrant mountain

the mountain of flowering trees

the woman with the nice smile

the ground starting to shake

---

a small village on Mars

a magical place

flying kites in the wind

---

twinkling stars above the sky

a secret place you can hide in

a bird's-eye view

your hammock, hanging between two palm trees

a haunted house with some ghosts

an Arctic expedition to the North Pole

---

a lizard with a fox tail

a room that holds a lot of memories

a procession where people sing

the moon, hanging in the sky like a sickle

a jumping heart

couples picnicking and dancing

shadowy trees

lion and dragon dances

a sleepy and quiet morning

a missing puzzle piece

the colorful reflection of fireworks in the water

houses that are stuck together

a footprint on a path

endless waves

lavish tuxedoes and extravagant hats

sun gleaming through the curtains

---

plum-shaped purple ears

a barrel of pistachios

---

music notes falling like raindrops

Mr. Potato walks to the store

a double-tailed rattlesnake | a ghost wearing a mask

a ball shaped like a diamond

Fred, the scooter-skateboarder

a villain with a dragon's head and a man's body

grasshopper pie

a car repair shop

a green and fluffy house

---

people with dresses and wings

---

a very fast shrimp

the inside of your private jet

a flock of flying lizards

a magic potion

a villain who lives underground

---

an animal with cheetah spots, great white teeth, and eagle wings

a pond full of ducks

a scary house

happily ever after

---

a ghost with big teeth

---

a dragon lying on the floor

eyeball soup

a big, dead palm tree

picking blackberries on the hill

a kitten sleeping in a cloud

a moving forest

---

molten hot weather

Super Girl

a police officer in a town of octopuses

---

a walking potato

the inside of a burrito

---

eight magic gods

a girl throwing smashed blueberries into the sky

a snow monster taking blue flowers

a brave warrior

red tomatoes that feel like pillows

a very sunny day with no clouds

a red Komodo dragon

a ref blowing the whistle

a superhero with superpowers

a superhero school

a super sparkly, pink dress

a colorful parrot

a junkyard

a monkey peeling a banana

a cactus as spiky as a porcupine

a three-foot pool of water

a swimmer holding a waterproof flashlight

an orange tree

the tiniest bug in the world

a balloon wearing a sombrero

a medium-size fish

flowers made of lollipops

a scary animal

black bear that weighs three hundred pounds

a killer whale

---

a time machine

a balloon tied to a chair

a string cheese castle

a carrot-broccoli superhero

a sugar skull

a cave

an old and scary mansion

a pirate mermaid

---

an octopus stuck inside a boat

a half dolphin, half gorilla

a river separating two towns

a two-headed vampire

a fireball

a dog wearing a jersey

pancakes raining from the sky

a one-eyed monster

a tornado

a farm

a chicken army

a deflated soccer ball

a huge diamond

a cotton candy castle

a beach in wintertime

a secret lab

the center of the Earth

a monkey scientist with three eyes

a teenage tree

a knight with wooden armor

a half raccoon, half iguana

a forest

a dragon in the sky

a raccoon that is turning into another animal

a potion bottle

a potion shop

a palm tree forest

a wizard worm

a thunderstorm

---

a sand castle

a jet pack

a talking book

someone playing video games while eating chips

shrimp chips

a pizza delivery girl

a cheetah-human

a marathon runner

the Golden Gate Bridge

a troll under a bridge

a jewelry store

a fairy-tale library

shark-infested waters

a three-foot-tall basketball player

an animal morphing machine

an old pirate ship

a 3-D map of your home

an aquarium

---

a sleeping boy

a griffin

an owl-koala

an alien with a squid head

a cowfish

a penguin catching fish

a pirate fox

cuckoo clocks

a big pearl in an oyster

a baby whale

a balloon robot

a mini golf course

a windmill

a grandfather clock

mini people living inside a clock

---

a pocket watch

an explorer of the jungle

a donut truck

a movie theater

_____

a zombie-troll

_____

a swan

a giraffe

a vampire giraffe

rainbow lollipops

the beach on a rainy day

a creepy graveyard

a fairy bat

a squirrel chasing a fairy

polka-dot flowers

a full moon

playing volleyball on the beach

a concert on the beach

a soccer team of ants

a magical lollipop wand

a yellow duck

a sparkling dress

disco dancing

a golden egg

a wild rainforest

a jungle boy

a T. rex living in a jungle

a three-headed dragon

a house painter

an underwater amusement park

a pirate-themed roller coaster

an underwater waterslide

a sunken skyscraper

a sea monster

robot tacos

bird–watching

a dolphin playing in the water

a burning candle

the best burger on earth

pets eating food

a taco monster

---

a series of islands

---

an active volcano

a plumber

a barber

a spaceship

a baby with a slingshot

you, as twins

---

a circus scene

a pizza box

a moat

a bookstore

a secret treasure hidden on a planet in outer space

an animal eating a popsicle

you, as a statue

a dog getting out of his leash

a woolly mammoth

an ice volcano

a snowman

an evil scientist

a warm winter scarf

a winning trophy

a fish family

a submarine in the sea

a cool place

creepy masks

a squirrel, who was really a witch

a cat party

things that howl in the forest

a leafy neighborhood

the funniest family ever

a mom who is like sunshine

two gigantic ogres

a very fast caterpillar

a crazy scientist

lemon trees

strawberry plants

---

a neighborhood that smells sweet

---

a cheetah and a leopard

the middle of a seaweed forest

a mysterious man in an overcoat

a monkey and a polar bear

a monster that can jump really high

a girl collecting seashells

a big crystal room

the inky black waters of Scotland

lollipop trees and cotton candy clouds

---

the freezing winter wind

a cowboy's lasso

a seagull flying into fog

a jungle of rebar and flowers

the shadow of your fingers

the sky's tears

---

the Alien Pizzeria

Lepus the deer

twenty kangaroos

---

pasta with broccoli and peppers

---

a cupcake dress

a dream

a cowboy snowman

rain making a lot of noise

a fat snail

a flying hamster

a blataphant (half elephant, half bat)

an imaginary world

a tea cup concert

a world made up of sticks

an alphabet house

a spaghetti maze

summer sadness

a broken daydream

happiness in a bottle

sticks and stones

a puddle of love

a sneaky animal stealing dessert

a family of robots on vacation

a monster sports team winning the championship

another planet where everything is one color

the saddest animal on the planet

dinner at the circus

a puzzle that can't be solved

a very friendly spider

---

shoes for walking on clouds

prehistoric video games

books for dogs

a dog in a frilly tutu

a dog walking a human

a man wearing spectacles with a beard made from beetles

two fish kissing

a rabbit in cowboy boots

a tiger who lives on a telephone pole

a witch who likes to knit

cats wrapped around hair like a towel wrapped around wet hair after a shower

---

a hippopotamus skipping in a park

---

a flower from another planet

a giant squid

a seal in a sweater

a sword made out of water

you and your best friends

a pirate chicken

balloons in animal shapes

a treasure map

sunrise over the horizon

a pirate sloth climbing a mast

a monster van

your favorite food

your name, using real-world objects instead of letters

your favorite animal if it were a robot

a sad bird

---

a happy egg

people living inside cotton candy

---

a hot dog chandelier

a pepperoni pizza professor

a dust-bunny wizard

a cyclops working his day job

a hot dog animal

a laser bee

a tree with a secret door

a guitar that plays itself

a campsite

---

a pirate boyfriend

---

an ice-skating rink

buried treasure

a pyramid

a blue stone

an old-timey deep-sea diver

a whale carrying a city

a butterfly

any corner of the room you are in

a space dolphin

a jellyfish

a surprise in a snow globe

a comet or meteor

a monster slug

numbers having a party

a bicycle

a map of the United States from memory (no references!)

an underground ant metropolis

what you ate for breakfast

the worst meal you ever had

a ghostly husky named Cody

bungee jumping off Mount Everest at night

a yellow-curry smoke

a statue that feels lonely

a fabulous, stupendous, spectacular, absolutely excellent day

---

a ghost that's old and rusty

you, when you're eighty years old

a croaking frog

December 31 at 4:44 a.m.

a hat falling off a cliff and onto a child's head

---

an island surrounded by a sea of juice

---

a whispering door

a thousand sapphire birds taking flight

a delicate hand

a spicy salsa pool

a telescope toppling over in the wind

---

sitting out on the balcony, feet on the railing

you, as a spy

secret agents setting a trap

---

memories that are too loud

Wally, the dancing cat

a plumed hat

plastic heart-shaped sunglasses

a hairless dog named Fluffy

a parking lot where there is nowhere to park

conversations with seagulls

a delightful, ruby-eyed snake

a pillow fight